Martín Dihigo

THE GREATEST BASEBALL PLAYER YOU'VE NEVER HEARD OF

Written
DARREN LÓPEZ

Illustrated
ERIC KITTELBERGER

HAVANA
MATANZAS
Martin's Home
SANTA CLARA
ISLA DE LA JUVENTUD
SANTIAGO DE CUBA
GUANTANAMO

For the Dihigo family
and all the Negro
League players who
paved the way.
-DL

For D., M., M. with
all my love.
-EK

Everyone has heard of the legendary homeruns of Babe Ruth, the amazing resilience of Jackie Robinson, the heart of gold of Roberto Clemente, and the beautiful swing of Ken Griffey Jr.

JACKIE RO

MARTÍN DIHIGO
Left Field

MARTÍN DIHIGO
Center Field

MARTÍN DIHIGO
Shortstop

MARTÍN DIHIGO
Third Base

But have you heard of a ball player that excelled in EVERY position, managed the team, was inducted into seven different halls of fame and who some have said was the "greatest baseball player to ever live?" All of which earned him the nickname "El Maestro" (the master) in Mexico and "El Inmortal" (the immortal) in his home country of Cuba. This is the story of Martín Dihigo.

MARTÍN DIHIGO
Right Field
MARTÍN DIHIGO
Second Base
MARTÍN DIHIGO
First Base
MARTÍN DIHIGO
Pitcher
MARTÍN DIHIGO
Catcher

Martín Dihigo was born in a humble sugar mill town in the province of Matanzas, Cuba. He was very proud of his father being a Mambí – a Cuban freedom fighter against Spanish colonial rule. His father wanted him to work a trade, but Martín's passion was baseball. Channeling the Mambí spirit and pride inherited from his father, he grew up living and breathing the game of baseball. The Mambí culture continued to live through him through his determination and kindness.

His passion for baseball bloomed into a professional career at the age of 16 when he played for Havana in the Cuban baseball league. Even with a tall, slim, and muscular build, he was still a boy playing amongst grown men. Batting from both sides of the plate and thriving in all positions, Martín's baseball versatility and talents immediately caught the attention of fans and scouts. A superstar was in the making! At the age of 17, he played for the Cuban Stars which barnstormed* the east coast of the U.S. in the Negro Leagues.*

* **Barnstorming:** *A word used to describe traveling between different locations to play against different teams.*

* **Negro Leagues:** *The Negro Leagues was an organized baseball league for Black baseball players that existed between 1920-1960.*

Dihigo was a great hitter from
both sides of the plate.

Martín's international success meant that he spent winters playing in Cuba and summers in the United States. He became a feared fastball hitter, but pitchers soon found his weakness versus the curveball. The Mambí spirit rose again motivating Martín to work fiercely against this limitation. Day in and day out, his teammates would throw him curveballs during batting practice. His resilience and dedication helped turn him into a deadly curveball hitter and just a couple of years later he would become the best hitter in the Cuban, Mexican, and Negro Leagues.

Agility, amazing speed, athleticism, and a cannon of an arm caught the eyes of the coaches who experimented with Martín at each position. He fervently played wherever he was needed, and surpassed expectations at all of them!

In the United States, the Jim Crow laws troubled Martín as he was treated as a second-class citizen because of being Black. Throughout his travels in the U.S., these laws made it difficult for him to find a restaurant to eat at or a decent hotel to sleep in. He was very proud of being Black and his Mambí spirit of justice would speak out against these laws that didn't allow equal treatment for Blacks in the South. Even though racism was present in Cuba, there weren't laws that systematically furthered such inequities.

NO DOGS NEGROS MEXICANS
COLORED SERVE IN REAR
ING FOUNTAIN
COLORED
E PRO
GRO
11

NEW YORK
CUBAN

The inequalities and challenges he faced as a Black Cuban didn't prevent him from being successful. His passion and love for the game helped him rise above the difficulties. Martín struck out future Hall of Famers, turned double plays, and threw out runners from the outfield trying to get extra bases. He did it all!

Josh Gibson, the most feared slugger in the Negro Leagues.

According to Hall of Famer Rudy Johnson, one winter in Havana, Martín had a pregame throwing contest against a professional jai alai player who used his cesta to throw and hit the center-field fence on one hop. The Mambí spirit of determination took over Martín as his ball soared over the fence, a throw easily more than 400 feet!

Martín excelled in the Negro Leagues and Cuban Leagues as a pitcher and position player throughout the 1920s and early 1930s. In México, Martín's passion and graceful skills all over the baseball diamond earned him the nickname "el Maestro" (the master) because he was considered a master of the game, dominating as a pitcher and feared as a hitter. In fact, Martín went on to pitch the first no-hitter in Mexican League history! In the 1938 season for the Rojos del Aguila Veracruz, he won eighteen games, lost two, allowing less than one run per game (ERA 0.90), and still ended the season with a batting average of .387! He also played against future Hall of Famers in the Dominican Republic and Venezuela.

Johnny Mize, Major League Baseball Hall of Famer, said that Martín Dihigo was the greatest baseball player to live. Mize was amazed Dihigo could play all the positions, hit from both sides of the plate, and manage the game.

Johnny Mize says ...
"THE GREATEST EVER!"

Martín was also known for his kindness.
He once helped future Hall of Famer
Minnie Minoso as a child get into the
stadium in Cuba by having him carry
his shoes and bat. Martín gave Minnie
some lifelong baseball advice that
Minnie later credited him to
help on his path to becoming
a baseball star.

MINNIE MINOSO IN A CHICAGO
WHITE SOX UNIFORM ON HIS
1954 BOWMAN BASEBALL CARD!

Martín's accomplishments have been recognized throughout the baseball world by being elected to seven baseball halls of fame including the National Baseball Hall of Fame, Cuban Baseball Hall of Fame, Mexican Baseball Hall of Fame, Venezuelan Baseball Hall of Fame, Dominican Baseball Hall of Fame, Buck Leonard First Baseman's Hall of Fame and the Hispanic Heritage Hall of Fame. This is how his Cuban nickname was earned — "El Inmortal (the immortal)." To be recognized by so many people in so many countries is how one becomes immortal. As fellow Hall of Famer, the great Buck Leonard said, "He was the greatest ballplayer of all time, black or white." His accomplishments speak for themselves, and every baseball fan should know his story.

29

AUTHORS NOTE*

On a blistering hot summer day in Ponce, Puerto Rico, I walked to a bench to get some shade and saw an elderly man sitting on the bench in a New York Yankees hat. It was Millito Navarro! A 102-year-old former Puerto Rican baseball player, he played for the NY Cubans in the late 20s, and has been involved in baseball for over 90 years. His memory was fresher than a 30-year-old. We sat down and spoke about baseball for about two hours. I asked him, "You have seen over a century of baseball – the Negro Leagues, the Major Leagues and all the Latin American Winter Leagues. You've seen Babe Ruth, Willie Mays, Ted Williams, Roberto Clemente. Who is the best baseball player you've ever seen?" He responded, "A Cuban ballplayer that did it all, Martín Dihigo." And that is what inspired my research for this book and motivated me to help Martín Dihigo continue to be "El Inmortal."

A special thanks to the Dihigo family and Foundation
Martín Dihigo Inc. for their blessing on this project.

WWW.FOUNDATIONMARTINDIHIGO.ORG

How did Martín's father's background help him as a baseball player?

How did Martín approach his weaknesses?

How did Martín feel about the Jim Crow laws?

What are some legendary feats accomplished by Martín?